Does Terrorism Influence Public Support for the Death Penalty?

Research on Public Policy Series

JAMIE L. FLEXON

LISA STOLZENBERG

STEWART J. D'ALESSIO

CHRISTOPHER DUSZKA

MARCO MUSCILLO

CONTENTS

ABSTRACT

It is well recognized that public views concerning the death penalty vary by the demographic characteristics of individuals and by contextual factors such as homicide rates, but much less is known as to whether shifts in public support for capital punishment are impacted by large-scale transient events such as terrorist attacks directed against the homeland. This study contributes to the extant literature by using longitudinal data drawn from the General Social Survey and the Uniform Crime Reports and a panel research design to determine empirically whether the coordinated terrorist attacks carried out on U.S. soil on September 11, 2001 (9/11) increased public support for the death penalty. Results show that the terrorist attacks perpetrated on 9/11 had little effect on amplifying public support for the death penalty. Such a finding suggests that public support for the death penalty is relatively stable over time and is not likely to be altered to any substantial degree by transient events such as acts of terrorism.

Keywords: Death Penalty, Terrorism, American Exceptionalism, Instrumental Perspective, Symbolic Perspective, 9/11

BACKGROUND

The Antiterrorism and Effective Death Penalty Act of 1996 (AEDPA) was signed into law by President William J. Clinton in response to the Oklahoma City bombing. Several years later in response to the 9/11 terrorist attacks, President George W. Bush secured passage of another piece of sweeping legislation directed at reducing terrorism when he signed the Uniting and Strengthening America by Providing Appropriate Tools Required to Intercept and Obstruct Terrorism Act of 2001 (USA PATRIOT Act). Both of these legislative acts exemplify efforts to quell terrorist activity by strengthening the government's investigatory ability and punitive response. Irrespective of their actual efficacy in protecting the populace against the specter of terrorism, these and other statutes attempt to send a symbolic message that the government can ameliorate terrorism by legislative efforts designed to more accurately identify terrorists before atrocities can be initiated and by the imposition of severe punitive sanctions such as the death penalty to deter or more appropriately punish those deserving.

Governmental legislative action intended to escalate the severity of punishment for terrorist activity is by no means uncommon and does not exist in a vacuum oblivious to public sentiment. Because penal legislation in the U.S. is subject to the vacillating temperament of the voting populace (i.e., American Exceptionalism), understanding the specific forces that drive penal preferences such as the death penalty is salient to ensure that policy is driven by something more than moral outrage. As Tonry (2004: 68) writes, "It is important to be sure that the reasons why punishment policies are to be made harsher are sound, and that they result from something other than raw emotion or short-term upset." However, while much is known about the character of death penalty supporters and opponents, far less is understood about shifts in public sentiment regarding the death penalty owning to larger, ephemeral events such as terrorist acts targeting American citizens within the homeland. While it is recognized that public sentiment concerning the death penalty varies by murder rates and other contextual factors (Baumer, Messner, and Rosenfeld 2003), additional potential influences on public support for the death penalty like 9/11 or other similar atrocities have yet to be scrutinized.

AMERICAN EXCEPTIONALISM

American exceptionalism is an explanation for the unique atmosphere of American politics and is best characterized as "a theory developed to explain certain features of the polity that are historic, persistent and widespread ..." (Garland 2005: 350). These unique traits of American ideology are theorized to play a noteworthy role in shaping politics and modern values. The U.S. was founded not by warring families nor was it built by an aristocracy (though it can be argued that the few who founded this nation were of a type of elite), but rather by the union of representatives of several governments seeking their independence from a nation rife with those very characteristics. This foundation, which was paved by "liberty, egalitarianism, individualism, populism, and laissez faire," separates Americans culturally from other Western nations (Poveda 2000: 254). These persistent traits are said to be attributed to the unique atmosphere of American politics and values that have been birthed by American culture and have persisted longer than many would have expected. These persistent traits, arising as early as the birth of this nation, such as being a frontier society having a "cultural mindset that his sympathetic to vigilantism" (particularly in the Southern states), and the absence of anti-aristocratic revolutions that would have developed status-consciousness of offenders and prisoners, improving their treatment, add to the unique atmosphere of American politics and culture that define American exceptionalism (Kugler, Funk, Braun, Gollwitzer, Kay, and Darley 2013: 1076; Whitman 2003). This attitude and culture of Americans is believed to contribute to a more punitive criminal justice system than any other Western nation (Steiker 2002: 103; Tonry 2001).

The modern approach to American exceptionalism holds that there is a qualitative difference in the approach to criminal justice sentencing in the U.S. that began in the mid-20th century (particularly in the 1960s and 1970s). This situation has promoted higher levels of incarceration, longer durations of imprisonment, and a greater use of the death penalty in recent years (1980s and 1990s) as compared to other Western nations. This kind of influence on the criminal justice system is partly due to the manipulation of public sentiment, which is commonly referred to as penal populism (Roberts, Stalans, Indermaur, and Hough 2002).

Penal populism is primarily used during election cycles by major political parties to sway public opinion. The focus here is that the promotion of "tough on crime" policies sways public opinion and support, leading to an increase in punishment. These discussions typically end with the promotion and acceptance or demotion and rejection of capital punishment by party front-runners. Steiker (2002: 111) attests to this climactic moment in politics by noting that the death penalty has served as "a focal point in electoral politics already organized around law and order." Very often the tough on crime proponent is the more appealing political candidate, eventually culminating in the imposition of legislation aimed at increasing the severity of criminal punishment.

If American exceptionalism is the influence of American ideology, culture, and sentiment in politics and legislation, how, then, can it increase punitive policies (capital punishment) when factoring in terrorism? Many policies have been enacted as a direct response to external threats, bypassing several safeguards and citizens' rights that are the bedrock of the American governmental system. The relocation of Japanese-Americans months after the attack on Pearl Harbor or the enactment of the PATRIOT Act as a reaction to the terrorist attacks on 9/11 are two examples of governmental responses to sudden and violent attacks against its citizenry. These responses are not completely rational, nor were they intended to be policies before such attacks had occurred, yet, they were accepted almost without question or regard for their intended audience (primarily American citizens). This urgency to retaliate to such attacks as a measure of precaution, leading to an eventual proactive assault on those responsible (i.e. executing terrorists on death row), is tantamount to a resurgence in a retributive form of justice and resulting from fear from unanticipated violent acts. The exceptionalism of the criminal justice system here may be characterized by a society that accepts the sanction of capital punishment in greater numbers after recent terrorist events have transpired.

It is also important to recognize that the death penalty is argued to hold prominence as it serves as an indicator for a myriad of criminal justice related views (Fitzgerald and Ellsworth 1984). It represents the most punitive response that the government can hand down, and as such, the death penalty is argued to be a hallmark attitude of criminal justice related matters (e.g., Fitzgerald and Ellsworth 1984; Young 2004). Capital punishment, however, also serves as an indicator of political-social ideology (Tyler and Weber 1982). In light of the above, it could be argued that the death penalty may be serving a pragmatic role or a more symbolic one. With this in mind, further attention is given to this distinction and the nature of death penalty support in a population deemed exceptional.

THE DEATH PENALTY AND PUBLIC SAFETY

Two perspectives have been offered for why an individual decides to support capital punishment (e.g., Maxwell and Rivera-Vazquez 1998; Tyler and Weber 1982). Instrumental theory proffers that an individual supports the death penalty out of a desire to lower the crime rate (Baumer et al. 2003). This desire to attenuate criminal activity through the use of the death penalty results from an individual being fearful of crime, from the view that crime is widespread, and from the belief that the death penalty is an effective crime deterrent. A number of studies lend empirical credence to this position. For instance, Thomas and Fosters (1975) found that support for the death penalty among Floridians was associated strongly with the fear of crime, the perception that the crime rate was high, and the belief that the death penalty was effective in deterring crime. Although beyond the geographic scope of the present study, in a survey of Canadians, Vidmar (1974) found similar results in that 42 percent of respondents supported the death penalty for its supposed deterrent effects. National support for the death penalty is also correlated with national crime rates. Public support for the death penalty has been observed to rise in surveys like the Gallup poll when the national crime rate rises, especially when homicide rates rise. Jacobs and Carmichael (2004), for instance, found that jurisdictions with the highest crime rates were more apt to sentence offenders to death.

Instrumental theory also argues that an individual's opinion on the use of the death penalty is subject to modification depending on environment factors and on the gathering of new information. Thus, it stands to reason that acts of terrorism should result in the targeted population becoming more supportive of the death penalty due to an escalation in the fear of being victimized by a terrorist act and/or from the specter of terrorism becoming more pronounced. Citizens should be more willing to support the use of severe punitive punishments like the death penalty in the hope that such measures will placate the terrorist threat.

Symbolic theory is a second perspective commonly advanced to explain why a person decides to support capital punishment (Stack 2003). This theory proffers that support for the death penalty is rooted in certain values or beliefs held by the individual (e.g., conservative, liberal, fundamentalist, etc.). These values and beliefs are often shaped by participation in political or religious organizations. For example, being politically conservative is associated with having a tough on crime view and could explain why Republicans generally tend to support the death penalty (See Jacobs and Carmichael 2002 for a discussion of the political sociology of the death penalty). Conservatives tend to believe that criminals are rational beings that can be deterred from committing crimes through the use of tough punitive measures like the death penalty. Their feeling is that public safety is more apt to be actualized by the use of punitive state sanctions than by social reforms and rehabilitation. They also feel that criminals deserve to be punished in a manner that is proportionate to the offense that they committed. The death penalty would be considered a punitive measure that is proportionate to offenses like homicide within this ideology. In support of this viewpoint, McCann (2008) demonstrated that conservative states utilized the death penalty more often than liberal states.

Additionally, high levels of societal threat were only observed to be associated with higher death penalty rates in conservative states.

Conversely, political liberals have a greater proclivity to be against the death penalty because they typically feel that social reforms are better than tough punitive measures in achieving public safety. According to their ideology, much of the criminality we experience is the result of an inegalitarian society. Thus, the most expedient way to attenuate criminality in society is to address the problem of inequality. Liberals also tend to be more optimistic in the belief that criminals can be rehabilitated, which combined with their general view that the death penalty is cruel, are less inclined to favor capital punishment. Support for the death penalty among liberals may also be lower as liberals are generally more empathetic and as a result are less apt to support harsher punitive sanctions (Unnever, Cullen, and Roberts 2005).

Religious ideology has a strong influence on an individual's opinion regarding the use of the death penalty. Support for the death penalty has been found to vary based on denomination. For example, Catholics are less likely to support the death penalty. This could be due to Catholics having consistent pro-life ethics. Support for the pro-life hypothesis comes from studies that have demonstrated that Catholics are more likely to simultaneously oppose the death penalty and abortion (Kelly and Kudlac 2000; Perl and McClintock 2001). However, more recent research supports the idea that is it the degree of religious fundamentalism that better elucidates the connection between religion and the death penalty by showing that protestant fundamentalists are generally more apt to support capital punishment (Applegate, Cullen, and Vander Ven 2000). A possible explanation is that protestant fundamentalism espouses bible literalism more so than most other Christian denominations. Research demonstrates that literal interpretation is associated with stronger support for the death penalty. To illustrate, Jacobs and Carmichael (2004) found that U.S. geographical regions with high membership in fundamentalist churches utilized the death penalty more frequently.

Under the symbolic theory, as opposed to instrumental theory, an individual's opinion on the use of capital punishment is likely to be stable and fixed throughout their lifetime. Changes in their environment and the addition of new information are unlikely to sway their opinion on the death penalty since opinion is dictated more by an individual's prevailing ideology. Therefore, according to the theory, acts of terrorism are unlikely to change an individual's opinion on the application of capital punishment as their ideology would make their beliefs on the use of capital punishment resistant to outside influences.

SUMMARY AND THE CURRENT STUDY

The primary purpose of terrorism, as its name implies, is to inflict a psychological impact, a terror, upon a targeted community through brutal acts of violence. Such acts resonate with a populace in many ways including through perceptions of risk and concern for continued threats of attack from hostile, external forces. It is reasonable to speculate that a heightened concern over the external and perceived threat of terrorist activity may influence the public's support for highly punitive responses and retaliatory action (Huddy et al. 2005). It is also plausible that the person desiring to inflict harm through the death penalty does so because he or she sees those being executed as the deserving party and themselves as the victim (Bowers and Pierce 2000), which is quite the opposite of what is intended by the policy. The populace may thus identify with the victims of terrorist acts. Though the community may be absent a means to inflict direct retaliatory action, a desire for state action through the death penalty, as a mechanism to vicariously satisfy a desire for vengeance, may be stimulated. In this way, the terrorist acts may have the effect of creating a desire for vengeance from the victims, direct and indirect, rather than simply instilling fear. Hence, the resulting impact of terrorism on public sentiments and sensibilities may be to amplify support for punitive state actions. The death penalty may serve as an indicator of this desire for retaliatory vengeance among the populace and increased levels of public support for the death penalty may be realized as a consequence of terrorist acts. In sum, terrorist acts may brutalize sensibilities of the populace by incensing the desire for lethal vengeance as the community comes to identify with the victims of terrorist atrocities. This position is consistent with the instrumental approach discussed earlier.

Support for the death penalty, for some individuals, is arguably nested in a desire to aid in public safety and protection. It is with this understanding that support for the death penalty may be serving as a proxy for individuals' concerns over public safety, which are heightened during the upheaval engendered by terrorist attacks. One hypothesis, then, is that when large scale violent events that threaten public safety transpire, shifts in support for this public policy will materialize. The intent and purpose of this study, then, is to determine if the terrorist acts that occurred on 9/11 influenced public support for the death penalty, which is considered a proxy for public punitiveness.

However, it is equally as likely that individuals hold to some prevailing ideology that dictates their views concerning capital punishment. Such postulates belong to symbolic theory which was discussed earlier. In accordance with this view, stability in views regarding the death penalty is to be expected and terrorist events should have no impact on feelings toward the death penalty. An individual's prevailing ideology would make beliefs concerning capital punishment resistant to outside environmental influences like terrorism. A null finding, then, would support the precepts of the symbolic perspective. The findings generated in this study should help elucidate which of these two perspectives holds the most validity.

DATA AND METHODS

The longitudinal data used in this study to evaluate the impact of the 9/11 terrorist attacks on public support for the death penalty were culled from the 1990 General Social Survey (GSS) and from the Uniform Crime Reports (UCR). These data were calibrated in two-year intervals for a total of 10 measurement periods based on data availability for the GSS. These 10 measurement periods encompass the following years: 1994, 1996, 1998, 2000, 2002, 2004, 2006, 2008, 2010, and 2012. We also aggregated the data at the regional level because region is the smallest geographical unit for which the GSS data are made available for secondary analysis and because support for capital punishment has been found to vary by region (Bohm 1998; Dieter 1996).

The 1990 GSS is a full-probability sample of English speaking, U.S. residents age 18 years and older living in households. The GSS employs face-to-face interviewing that takes place throughout February and March each year (Davis and Smith 1992). Subjects are asked a variety of questions concerning attributes, attitudes, and behaviors. A weight is available in the dataset allowing for inferences to be made at the individual-level since household is the unit of analysis for the survey. This weight was employed for this study. Adults living in institutions and group quarters are excluded from the survey (Davis and Smith 1992: 31). Participation rates for the GSS vary according to age group. Generally, the least represented age groups include 18 to 24 year olds and those 75 and older; those aged 25 to 64 are the most represented in the survey (Davis and Smith 1992). Issues that precluded respondent participation in the study included misspecification of sampling units, language problems, refusals to participate in the study, non-availability of respondents, and respondent illness (Davis and Smith 1992: 54-55).

The dependent variable used in this study is the percent of respondents in the GSS reporting support for the death penalty. Over 70% of the survey respondents on average favored the death penalty during the observation period.

Our independent variable of theoretical interest is the terrorist attacks that occurred on 9/11. This dummy variable is coded one for the years after 9/11 (2002-2012) and zero otherwise (1994-2001). If terrorist attacks on U.S. soil increase public support for the death penalty, the coefficient for the dummy coded 9/11 variable should be positive and statistically substantive. In the absence of a strong positive relationship, no impact of the 9/11 terrorist attacks on public support for the death penalty can be inferred.

Although our primary objective is to assess the influence of the 9/11 attacks on the public support for the death penalty, the multivariate panel model used here allows for an assessment of the influence of other potentially salient variables. If these additional variables are not taken into account, any observed relationship between the 9/11 terrorist attacks and public support for the death penalty might be spurious. These aggregate control variables include the murder rate, percent of respondents identifying themselves as politically conservative, percent of Republican respondents, percent of religious fundamentalist respondents, average age of respondent, percent male respondents, and percent white respondents.

We used UCR data to control for the murder rate within the nine regional geographical areas for each of the years being studied because research shows that crime levels play an important role in determining patterns of support for the death penalty (Baumer et al. 2003; Jacobs and Carmichael 2004). The murder rate variable was created by dividing the number of murders each year by the regional population and multiplying by 100,000. The average murder rate for the nine regions was about six homicides per 100,000 population.

Two other control variables of potential salience are whether a survey respondent considers himself or herself to be politically conservative and whether the respondent is a Republican. Prior research finds that political conservatives and Republicans tend to have a favorable opinion of the death penalty (Sarat 2001). Eighteen percent of the respondents captured by the GSS considered themselves to be politically conservative, whereas 26% indicated that they were Republicans.

Religious ideology is also speculated to have a strong influence on an individual's opinion of the death penalty. Research finds that religious fundamentalists tend to be more apt to support the death penalty (Applegate et al. 2000; Jacobs and Carmichael 2004). Twenty nine percent of the respondents surveyed considered themselves to be religious fundamentalists. Research also suggests that older individuals (Flexon 2012) and whites tend to have more favorable views of the death penalty (Barkan and Cohn 1994; Cochran and Chamlin 2006; Flexon 2012; Peffley and Hurwitz 2007). The average age of a respondent was 45 years old. Approximately 80% of the respondents were white. The means, standard deviations, and definitions for all of the variables used in the study are reported in Table 1.

TABLE 1

Means, standard deviations, and definitions for the variables used in the analysis.

	Mean	SD	Definition
Death penalty	0.76	7.19	Percent supporting the death penalty.
9/11 attacks	.60	.49	Coded 1 for time periods occurring after the 9/11 attacks (2002-12), 0 otherwise.
Murder rate	5.69	1.95	Murder and non-negligent manslaughter rate per 100,000 population.
Politically conservative	8.01	6.12	Percent politically conservative or strongly conservative.
Republican	6.51	5.16	Percent Republican.
Religious fundamentalist	9.51	15.39	Percent fundamentalist in religious beliefs.
Age	5.14	2.11	Average age.
Male	5.79	3.99	Percent male.
White	0.23	8.63	Percent white.

NOTE: Data encompass nine U.S. regions (New England, Mid Atlantic, East North Central, West North Central, South Atlantic, East South Central, West South Central, Mountain, and Pacific) for 1994, 1996, 1998, 2000, 2002, 2004, 2006, 2008, 2010, and 2012.

RESULTS

We estimated two panel equations using LIMDEP (Greene 2007), whereby all nine regional districts (i.e., New England, Mid Atlantic, East North Central, West North Central, South Atlantic, East South Central, West South Central, Mountain, and Pacific) were treated as distinct observations to estimate the effect of the 9/11 terrorist attacks on public support for the death penalty. This type of analytic design is ideally suited for studying both the temporal and spatial patterns of public support for the death penalty because it can analyze multiple units across multiple time periods. This methodological strategy accounts for both cross-sectional and temporal complications of the data by enabling the consideration of variation across both region and time. We are thus able to account for region-specific variables that may explain variation in support for the death penalty that cannot be considered with a national time-series. Another advantage is that the analysis of panel data does not require a large number of temporal observations, which is typically needed in a time-series analysis. A two way random-effects model was used to estimate our equations because a Hausman test (Hausman and Taylor 1981), which evaluates whether a fixed effects model and random-effects model produce similar results, indicated that the random effects model was superior (Hausman test = 5.28, p = .626).

Table 2 reports the results of the two random-effects equations estimating the influence of the control variables and the 9/11 variable on public support for the death penalty. Model 1 is a baseline equation that includes the effects of only the control variables. The effect of the 9/11 terrorist attacks is then tested in Model 2 by adding the dummy coded intervention variable to the baseline equation. If the terrorist attacks that occurred on 9/11 increased public support for the death penalty, we would expect to find a substantive positive coefficient for the 9/11 intervention variable. In regards to the control variables, readers should place emphasis on the level of statistical significance, the direction of the coefficients, and the consistency of a variable's effect across the two estimated equations.

A visual inspection of Model 1 (baseline model) reveals that three of the seven control variables reach statistical significance in the equation. These three pronounced effects include the murder rate, whether the respondent was politically conservative, and whether the respondent was white. The R^2 for the model was .66. The dummy coded 9/11 variable was then added to the baseline equation in Model 2. The results for this model fail to show a statistically discernible relationship between the dummy coded variable measuring the 9/11 terrorist attacks and public support for the death penalty. The coefficient for the 9/11 variable is in the negative direction and it is not statistically significant at the .05 level of analysis. The effects of the control variables are compatible with those reported in Model 1. The murder rate, percent politically conservative and percent white all reach statistical significance in the equation. The R^2 for Model 2 (Table 2) remained unchanged at .66.

TABLE 2
Two way random-effects models estimating the impact of the 9/11 terrorist attacks on public support for the death penalty.

	Model 1 Controls Only		Model 2 With 9/11 Attacks	
	Coefficient	SE	Coefficient	SE
9/11 attacks	--	--	-1.741	2.387
Murder rate	1.789**	.603	1.679**	.646
Politically conservative	.311*	.140	.280*	.140
Republican	.153	.139	.172	.140
Religious fundamentalist	-.127	.096	-.127	.095
Age	-.496	.291	-.443	.307
Male	.143	.130	.149	.130
White	.266**	.099	.249**	.102
Constant	49.240	6.496	49.610	16.517
R^2	.657		.658	

NOTE: *$p \leq .05$, **$p \leq .01$, ***$p \leq .001$ (two-tailed tests).

DISCUSSION

This research is rooted in the larger inquiry concerning the drivers of capital punishment support. Hence, the purpose of this study was to discern if terrorist activities directed against the homeland, such as that of 9/11, influence public support for the death penalty. Two perspectives were used to conceptualize this question. One approach, the instrumental perspective, supports the notion that terrorist activities against the homeland will have a discernable impact on individuals' support for the death penalty. This approach argues that external, environmental factors impact a person's view about the death penalty as he or she gathers additional information. In the event of a terrorist attack, individuals may perceive a need to be more fearful of becoming a victim, either directly or indirectly, and therefore come to support the death penalty as a method to secure public safety and, as argued earlier, to seek retaliation. The alternative perspective, symbolic theory, postulates that terrorist attacks should have no discernable effect on death penalty support. The findings generated in this study showed that symbolic theory was better able to explain support for capital punishment as some prevailing ideology held by an individual like conservatism explained support for the death penalty while the terrorist attacks carried out on 9/11 did not.

In line with the symbolic approach, consistency in support for the death penalty is expected as people tend to be stable in their worldviews and ideology being somewhat inoculated against temporal, external influences. According to this view, then, stability in death penalty support should not be altered by transient events because an individual's prevailing ideology (i.e., conservative) or world view is resistant to such external influences. The significance of the crime rate in explaining death penalty support is arguably more in line with the instrumental perspective. However, it can be argued using the instrumental approach that environmental considerations such as the crime rate, which tend to be more stable over time, do not serve the function of being new, informative events. Within the instrumental theoretical framework, terrorist activity should have an impact on death penalty support based in part on its transient and punctuated nature.

Nevertheless, contrary to this assertion, our findings act to buttress symbolic theory. When the dummy variable for 9/11 was added to the main model of our analysis (Table 2), no discernable impact of this variable was observed on death penalty support. One can interpret this null effect as empirical evidence supporting the assertion that the 9/11 terrorist attacks had little effect on public opinion regarding the death penalty after accounting for other factors. Apparently, the fear of being a potential victim of a terrorist attack is not compelling enough to be a noteworthy factor in motivating people to amplify their support for capital punishment.

Our results also showed that political conservatism, which serves as a pre-existing ideological perspective, is salient in explaining support for the death penalty. This link between conservatism and support for capital punishment is consistent with the findings of others (Jacobs and Carmichael 2002; Sarat 2001) and further buttresses the symbolic approach evaluated here. As discussed earlier, symbolic theory recognizes that people hold to certain ideological perspectives, which then shape their position on a number of things including policy. Such values are further informed by participation in or identification with political or religious organizations. Our findings highlight that the politically conservative favor such things as retributive ideals and more punitive sanctions than their liberal counterparts independently of the 9/11 intervention. Thus, this finding bolsters the conclusions stemming from the null result produced in this study by showing that a pre-existing worldview remains a consistent driver of death penalty support, which again, is in line with symbolic theory.

FUTURE RESEARCH AND CONCLUSION

Although we believe that we have advanced knowledge with respect to our research question, our work can be improved. First, our analyses are performed at the aggregate level. Although appropriate and we would expect to see an influence at this level of analyses, it does not discount the idea that some impact from terrorist activities on death penalty support is being realized at the individual level. Hence, researchers may seek to further investigate this question at the individual level of analysis. In addition, we only evaluated one terrorist event, that of 9/11, on support for the death penalty. We chose this event for several reasons, including the magnitude of atrocities and lives lost on U.S. soil, the infamy and public awareness of the attack, and the multiple locations of the attack. Other researchers may wish to examine the potential impact of other terrorist attacks against the U.S. on support for the death penalty. In line with this prior suggestion, researchers may wish to scrutinize a more extensive time-frame than that used here.

In conclusion, we set out to answer whether terrorist events, such as that of 9/11, had a discernable impact on death penalty support. Our research suggests that it does not. Rather individuals are already vested in a prevailing perspective that informs their view concerning the death penalty, which are resistant to punctuated, external influences such as terrorist attacks. Our findings, as that of others, favored a more symbolic perspective (e.g., Tyler and Weber 1982). While other researchers are encouraged to revisit this question, we believe that we have furthered this area of research, which is nested within the broader question asking what influences public support for the death penalty.

REFERENCES

Applegate, B.K., Cullen, F.T., & Vander Ven, T. (2000). Forgiveness and fundamentalism: Reconsidering the relationship between correctional attitudes and verdicts. Criminology, 38, 719-754.

Barkan, S.E., & Cohn, S.F. (1994). Racial prejudice and support for the death penalty by Whites. Journal of Research in Crime and Delinquency, 31, 202-209.

Baumer, E. P., Messner, S. F., & Rosenfeld, R. (2003). Explaining spatial variation in support for capital punishment: A multilevel analysis. American Journal of Sociology, 108(4), 844-875.

Bohm, R.M. (1998). American death penalty opinion: Past, present, and future. In J. R. Acker, R.M. Bohm, and C.S. Lanier (Eds.), America's experiment with capital punishment: Reflections on the past, present, and future of the ultimate penal sanction, (pp. 25-76). Durham, NC: Carolina Academic Press.

Bowers, W. J., & Pierce, G. L. (1980). Deterrence or brutalization: What is the effect of executions? Crime & Delinquency, 26(4), 453-484.

Cochran, J.K., & Chamlin, M.B. (2006). The enduring racial divide in death penalty support. Journal of Criminal Justice, 34, 85-99.

Davis, J.A., & Smith, T.W. (1992). The NORC general social survey: A user's guide. Newbury Park, CA: Sage Publications, Inc.

Dieter, R.C. (1996). Twenty years of capital punishment: A re-evaluation. The Death Penalty Information Center.

http://www.deathpenaltyinfo.org/node/592

Fitzgerald, R., & Ellsworth, P. C. (1984). Due process vs. crime control: Death qualification and jury attitudes. Law and Human Behavior, 8(1-2), 31-51.

Flexon, J. L. (2012). Racial disparities in capital sentencing: Prejudice and discrimination in the jury room. El Paso, TX: LFB Scholarly Publishing.

Garland, D. (2005). Capital punishment and American culture. Punishment and Society, 7(4), 347-376.

Greene, W. H. (2007). LIMDEP, version 9.0. New York, NY: Econometric Software.

Hausman, J. A., & Taylor, W. E. (1981). Panel data and unobservable individual effects. Econometrica, 49, 1377-98.

Huddy, L., Feldman, S., Taber, C., & Lahav, G. (2005). Threat, anxiety, and support for antiterrorism policies. American Journal of Political Science, 49, 593-608.

Jacobs, D., & Carmichael, J.T. (2002). The political sociology of the death penalty: A pooled time-series analysis. American Sociological Review, 67, 109-131.

Jacobs, D., & Carmichael, J. T. (2004). Ideology, social threat, and the death sentence: Capital sentences across time and space. Social Forces, 83(1), 249-278.

Kelly, J. R., & C. Kudlac. (2000). Pro-life, anti-death penalty? America, April 1, 6-8.

Kugler, M. B., Funk, F., Braun, J., Gollwitzer, M., Kay, A. C., & Darley, J. M. (2013). Differences in punitiveness across three cultures: A test of American exceptionalism in justice attitudes. The Journal of Criminal Law and Criminology, 103(4), 1071-1113.

Maxwell, S. R., & Rivera-Vazquez, O. (1998). Assessing the instrumental and symbolic elements in attitudes toward the death penalty using a sample of Puerto Rican students. International Journal of Comparative and Applied Criminal Justice, 22(2), 329-339.

McCann, S. J. (2008). Societal threat, authoritarianism, conservatism, and US state death penalty sentencing (1977-2004). Journal of Personality and Social Psychology, 94(5), 913.

Peffley, M., & Hurwitz, J. (2007). Persuasion and resistance: Race and the death penalty in America. American Journal of Political Science, 51, 996-1012.

Perl, P., & McClintock, J. S. (2001). The Catholic "consistent life ethic" and attitudes toward capital punishment and welfare reform. Sociology of Religion, 62(3), 275-299.

Poveda, T. G. (2000). American exceptionalism and the death penalty. Social Justice, 27(2), 252-267.

Roberts, J. V., Stalans, L. J., Indermaur, D., & Hough, M. (2002). Penal populism and public opinion: Lessons from five countries. Oxford University Press.

Sandys, M., & Trahan, A. (2008). Life qualification, automatic death penalty voter status, and juror decision making in capital cases. Justice System Journal, 29(3), 385-395.

Sarat, A. (2001). When the state kills. Princeton, NJ: Princeton University Press.

Stack, S. (2003). Authoritarianism and support for the death penalty: A multivariate analysis. Sociological Focus, 36(4), 333-352.

Steiker, C. S. (2002). Capital punishment and American exceptionalism. Oregon Law Review, 81, 97-130.

Thomas, C. W., & Foster, S. C. (1975). A sociological perspective on public support for capital punishment. American Journal of Orthopsychiatry, 45(4), 641.

Tonry, M. (2004). Thinking about crime: Sense and sensibility in American penal culture. Oxford University Press, Inc.: New York, NY.

Tonry M. (2001). Punishment policies and patterns in western countries. In M. Tonry & R. S. Frase (Eds.), Sentencing and sanctions in western countries (pp. 3-28). New York: Oxford University Press.

Tyler, T. R., & Weber, R. (1982). Support for the death penalty; instrumental response to crime, or symbolic attitude? Law and Society Review, 17, 21-45.

Unnever, J. D., Cullen, F. T., & Roberts, J. V. (2005). Not everyone strongly supports the death penalty: Assessing weakly-held attitudes about capital punishment. American Journal of Criminal Justice, 29(2), 187-216.

U.S. Census Bureau. A–27 Census 2000 Geographic Terms and Concepts, U.S. Census Bureau, Census 2000.
http://www.census.gov/geo/www/tiger/glossry2.pdf

Vidmar, N. (1974). Retributive and utilitarian motives and other correlates of Canadian attitudes toward the death penalty. Canadian Psychologist/Psychologie Canadienne, 15(4), 337-356.

Whitman, J.Q. (2003). Harsh justice: Criminal punishment and the widening divide between America and Europe. New York: Oxford University Press.

Young, R. L. (2004). Guilty until proven innocent: Conviction orientation, racial attitudes, and support for capital punishment. Deviant Behavior, 25(2), 151-167.

APPENDIX

The GSS scheme for region comes from the U.S. Census Bureau. The breakdown of US Census Bureau regions by division and State is provided in Table A1.

TABLE A1
Breakdown of the US Census Bureau regional designation by division and state.

Northeast Region	Midwest Region
New England Division: Maine, New Hampshire, Vermont, Massachusetts, Rhode Island, Connecticut	*East North Central Division:* Ohio, Indiana, Illinois, Michigan, Wisconsin
Middle Atlantic Division: New York New Jersey, Pennsylvania	*West North Central Division:* Minnesota, Iowa, Missouri, North Dakota, South Dakota, Nebraska, Kansas
South Region	West Region
South Atlantic Division: Delaware, Maryland, District of Columbia, Virginia, West Virginia, North Carolina, South Carolina, Georgia, Florida	*Mountain Division:* Montana, Idaho, Wyoming, Colorado, New Mexico, Arizona, Utah, Nevada
East South-Central Division: Kentucky, Tennessee, Alabama, Mississippi	*Pacific Division:* Washington, Oregon, California, Alaska, Hawaii
West South-Central Division: Arkansas, Louisiana, Oklahoma, Texas	

NOTE: Excerpt altered for formatting. A–27 Census 2000 Geographic Terms and Concepts, U.S. Census Bureau, Census 2000.
http://www.census.gov/geo/www/tiger/glossry2.pdf

ABOUT THE AUTHORS

Jamie L. Flexon, Lisa Stolzenberg and Stewart J. D'Alessio are professors and Christopher Duszka and Marco Muscillo are graduate students in the School of International and Public Affairs at Florida International University. Direct correspondence to Jamie L. Flexon, Department of Criminal Justice, Florida International University, 11200 SW 8th Street - PCA 366A, Miami, FL 33199. E-mail: flexonj@fiu.edu.

www.ingramcontent.com/pod-product-compliance
Lightning Source LLC
Chambersburg PA
CBHW071344290326
41933CB00040B/2257